T0195827

GRADES 5-8

THE STOCK MARKET Game

A SIMULATION OF STOCK MARKET TRADING

11-21 → WALL ST

WRITTEN BY DIANNE DRAZE

ILLUSTRATED BY MARY LOU JOHNSON

First published in 2005 by Prufrock Press Inc.

Published in 2021 by Routledge
605 Third Avenue, New York, NY 10017
2 Park Square, Milton Park, Abingdon, Oxon OX14 4RN

Routledge is an imprint of the Taylor & Francis Group, an informa business

ISBN: 9781593631383 (pbk)

DOI: 10.4324/9781003238935

Contents

Introduction

Why Study the Stock Market?

The stock market is in the news every day, and even those people who do not personally trade securities or intend to make a fortune by trading stocks, have an interest in knowing something about the market. Most retirement funds are invested in stocks. Individual retirement accounts can be and often are invested in mutual funds. Most large companies offer their employees profit-sharing in the form of stock ownership. The strength of our nation's largest companies, and consequently the economic vitality of the nation, is intricately intertwined with what happens in the stock market. To get a clear picture of this, we need only recall the devastating shock wave that went through all areas of the economy when the stock market crashed during the 1930s.

By giving students an understanding of the stock market, then, we are preparing them to deal knowledgeably with an area of our society that has a vast effect on their lives. Whether or not they choose in later life to trade stocks on an individual basis, they will at least have the knowledge that will enable them to understand this aspect of the economy and how their personal economic pictures are affected by the larger economic landscape.

About This Book

The Stock Market Game is three books rolled into one. The first part of the book is an explanation of stocks, stock prices, stock markets, buying and selling stocks, and forces that affect stock prices. Each topic includes a reproducible information sheet and an activity, either in the form of a project or a worksheet.

• Short Version

The second part of the book is a mini-simulation that is designed to be used in classrooms where you cannot allocate several months to follow the stock market. This shorter version can also be used as an introduction to the longer game. It lasts about five days, and in this time, students can have enough experience with buying and selling stocks that they will understand how the real stock market works. In this shorter version students are given several fictional companies. Each day the instructor provides stock prices and news reports regarding these companies. Students can easily see the relationship between the news and the stock prices.

• Long Version

The longer version of the game uses many of the same rules and record forms as the shorter version, but it allows students to buy and sell stocks of actual companies and relies on actual stock prices from the stock exchanges and NASDAQ. The text gives information on twelve well-known companies. Students may choose stocks for companies other these twelve if they wish, but they need to know something about the companies and they need to have access to current prices.

If you choose to do this longer version, you may wish to have students start several weeks before the actual trading begins by selecting a company they find interesting and sending for information about that company. In this way, if they later choose to invest in this company, they will already have the information at hand.

For this longer version, you will need to allocate time over a period of several months. It is not necessary (or even advisable) to trade stocks every day during this time. Limiting trading days to once a week is adequate. With this time schedule students will study the stocks over a long enough period to see how market forces and news affect stock prices, but they will not have to devote time on a daily basis to check prices and trade. There is a fair amount of record keeping involved in the game, so this can take up a large part of class time if it is done on a more frequent schedule.

Points and Prices

Stock prices are quoted in points. One points equals one dollar. Historically each point was divided into eighths and prices were quoted in fractions. In the summer of 1997, the New York Stock Exchange, under pressure from various groups, including the government, made the big decision to convert prices from fractions to decimals. The plan was that prices would initially be changed from eighths to sixteenths and eventually decimals. Because stock trading is a huge network that includes not only the stock exchanges (there are nine of them), but also computer trading networks, the internal workings of companies that are listed on the stock exchanges, and stockbrokers, it was decided to phase in this change over a period of several years. The goal was to have the New York Stock Exchange convert its prices by the summer of 1998 and to have all aspects of the stock trading network working with decimals by the year 2002. Some newspapers began immediately quoting prices in decimals, but it is anticipated that some segments may take longer than predicted to make the change to decimals.

Depending on when you pick up this study unit and decide to begin the simulation, your newspaper may be quoting prices in fractions (in either eighths or sixteenths) or in decimals.

All prices in this book are written in decimals. If you are working with prices that are in fractions, you will probably want to present a lesson on converting prices from fractions to decimals and then to dollars. You may want to instruct students on how to mathematically convert from fractions to decimals, or you may want to give them the following equivalents:

$1/16 = .0625$	$9/16 = .5625$
$1/8 = .125$	$5/8 = .625$
$3/16 = .1875$	$11/16 = .6875$
$1/4 = .25$	$3/4 = .75$
$5/16 = .3125$	$13/16 = .8125$
$3/8 = .375$	$7/8 = .875$
$7/16 = .4375$	$15/16 = .9375$
$1/2 = .5$	

Once the procedure for changing from fractions to decimals is established, you can then show students that:

$62\frac{1}{2}$ points = 62.50 points = \$62.50.

Give students several problems on which to practice this procedure. It is important that if you are working with fractions students understand how to go from prices quoted in fractions to the dollar equivalents.

Glossary of Terms

American Stock Exchange - a stock exchange in New York City. Most of the stocks on this exchange are relatively small companies.

assets - things that are owned by individuals or businesses that can be converted into cash, such as money in bank accounts, accounts receivable, land, buildings, fixtures, and machinery.

bear market - stock prices are falling.

blue chip stocks - high-priced common stocks that have been strong, profitable stocks for a long period of time.

bonds - certificates of ownership of a portion of a debt that is due to be paid by a government or corporation to an individual; usually bearing a fixed rate of interest.

bull market - stock prices are rising.

capital - the wealth, money or property owned by an individual or business.

capitalism - an economic system in which goods and services are produced by private individuals and groups who control the production, compete with one another, and whose goal is to make a profit.

capital gains - money that is made (a profit) by selling an asset like a home or stocks.

commission - the price a stock broker charges to take care of buying or selling stock.

common stock - fractional shares of ownership in a business; partial ownership of a corporation through the ownership of stocks. Most people who own stock, own common stock.

corporation - an organization created by law whose shareholders have limited legal and financial liability.

diversify - to buy a variety of stocks.

dividend - money from profits of a company that is paid to the stockholders. Payment can be in cash or stock shares and is usually paid quarterly.

Dow Jones Industrial Average - a measure of stock market prices based on thirty leading companies of the New York Stock Exchange.

incorporation - the process of forming a corporation-type ownership of a business. This establishes a standard unit of accounting that makes it possible to exchange units of ownership.

initial public offering - the first time a corporation's stock is offered for sale to the public.

initial value - the value of the stock when it is first offered for sale. The price of stock at this point is determined by the total assets of the company.

investment - the use of resources (capital) to create wealth.

investor - someone who uses his or her money to purchase stocks with the expectation of making a profit.

market value - the value of a business in terms of what it can be sold for on the open market.

mutual fund - a portfolio or selection of stocks that is owned by many shareholders and managed by a professional stock manager. It allows people to pool their money with other people to buy a variety of stocks. Each fund will have a stated purpose that will guide the manager in buying and selling stocks. **Share price** is the value of all the assets (stocks) divided by the number of shares.

NASDAQ - National Association of Securities Dealers Automated Quotations. This computerized network provides prices and trading for more than 5,000 over-the-counter stocks.

New York Stock Exchange - the largest stock exchange, located in New York City. Most of the companies on this exchange are larger companies with higher-priced stock.

over-the-counter (OTC) - stocks that are traded with individual investment firms rather than at major or regional exchanges. These stocks are "unlisted." Companies traded over-the-counter are usually small companies. There are approximately 20,000 OTC stocks that are traded via a computer-telephone network that allows dealers to communicate directly with one another.

par value - the value printed on the face of a stock or bond; the same as **face value**.

point - the measurement of the value of stocks, usually divided into eighths. One point equals one dollar.

portfolio - the group of stocks that you own.

price - what you pay for a stock. Prices are quoted in points, a system in which one point equals one dollar. The price is determined by supply and demand. If there are only a few bidders or buyers for a stock, the price will be lower than when there are a lot of buyers.

price-earning ratio (P/E) - the price of the stock divided by its earnings for the last year. It is listed in most stock quotes and gives an idea of how cheap or expensive a stock is compared to other stocks.

or expensive a stock is compared to other stocks.

profit - money that is made or gained as a result of an investment.

securities - stocks and bonds.

Securities and Exchange Commission - a governmental agency that was established in 1934 to protect investors in securities (stocks and bonds). It registers all securities, licenses brokers, hears complaints, and penalizes people or companies who don't follow the rules.

share - one portion of ownership in a corporation.

shareholder - someone who owns shares of stock in a company.

speculation - to engage in business dealings that involve some risk in hopes of making a profit.

stocks - shares of ownership in a corporate or public body.

stockbroker - a professional who is licensed to buy and sell stocks.

stock exchange - a place where stocks and bonds are bought and sold.

stockholder - someone who owns shares of stock in a company; same as a shareholder.

stock certificate - a certificate that shows ownership of one or more shares of stock in a corporation.

stock split - when a company divides its stocks into smaller, more economical shares. If a stock splits 2 for 1, it means that stockholders get 2 shares for every one they own. The price of the new stock would be adjusted downward.

Stock Phrases

Name _____

Refer to the glossary and fill in the words that best complete each sentence.

Glenda Goodsense inherited some money when her uncle died. She decided that she wanted to become an _____ , so she could make more money with her inheritance. She decided to buy _____ in a company that she knew was a solid company and that paid out _____ each quarter. She visited her _____ , Molly Money, and told her what she wanted to do.

Molly advised Glenda to _____. "Don't put all your eggs in one basket," she said. She told Glenda how to put together a _____ of several stocks, and thereby reduce the risk of losing money if the market goes down (a _____ market).

Glenda chose four _____ _____ stocks of companies that were sound and had been leading companies for a long time. She also decided to buy three stocks that she found on the _____ , rather than listed on either the New York or American _____ _____. She asked Molly to check the current _____ for each stock and then decided to buy 100 _____ of each company. She paid the cost of buying the 700 shares plus a _____ to Molly for her services.

Glenda now had a _____ of stocks. Over the year she found that some of her stocks went up in price and some went down. One stock even _____ 3 for 2, so she ended up with more stocks than she started with. She was one happy _____.

Business Ownership

Types of Business Ownership

In a **capitalistic** economy, businesses are owned and operated by people (as opposed to the government). People engage in business because they want to make a **profit**. By investing **capital** (usually money, but sometimes property and equipment), they can start a business. The intent of these business owners is to use these assets to make goods or offer services that other people will buy. They then can make a profit.

There are three main types of ownership of businesses. They are:

■ Sole Proprietorship

These businesses are owned and operated by one person (though the owner may hire employees to do some of the work). It is the most widespread form of small business ownership.

■ Partnership

These businesses are owned by two or more people who are co-owners of the business. In most cases, they share the expenses, the work, and the profits from the business.

■ Corporation

A corporation is a legal entity. It is an association of individuals created by law that has powers and liabilities independent of its members. Legal papers must be filed with the state in which a business operates before it can become a corporation. Most businesses do not begin as corporations. Sole proprietorships and partnerships may eventually change the ownership to a corporation because of legal or economic reasons or because they want to raise capital by selling shares of the business. Forming a corporation is expensive and legally complicated.

Corporate Ownership

Corporations are owned by people who own stock in the business (stockholders). Some corporations may have many shareholders, and some may have only a few owners. In some corporations, the person or persons who started the business may own all the stocks. Other corporations may offer to sell stock in their business to other individuals. This is usually done when there is a need to raise money so the business can make more products or expand what they are presently doing. If the shares in the business are sold to other people, the sale of these shares is regulated by the Securities and Exchange Commission.

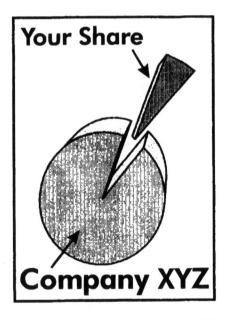

Your Share

Company XYZ

What Are Stocks?

Stocks are shares of ownership of a corporate-owned business. If you own a stock, you are a part-owner in the business. **Common stocks** are the kind of stocks that most people own. If a business has issued 10 stocks and you own 1 of them, you are a one-tenth owner in that business. If it makes a profit, you will share in that profit. If the company loses money, your stock will be worth less than the price you paid for it originally. You can attend stockholders' meetings and vote for the board of directors. You can sell your stocks (or part ownership) at any time.

Something To Do

- *List at least three businesses in your community that are most likely sole proprietorships.*
- *List at least three businesses in your community that are most likely partnerships.*
- *List at least three businesses in your community that are most likely corporations.*
- *Look at the business section of the newspaper and find the stock listings. List five companies with which you are familiar.*

Stock Prices

Business owners usually will decide to "go public" or to sell stock in their business to other people when they need to raise money to expand the business or to fund new endeavors. They divide their business ownership into pieces (shares) and offer these for sale to other people. When people buy the stocks, the money from the sale is then available for the company to use to build new plants, install up-to-date machinery, develop new products, or do more advertising.

Initial Prices

When a business first offers its stocks for sale to the public it is called an **initial stock offering**. The price of the stock is based on the assets of the business (money, buildings, machinery, and property) divided by the number of stocks. For instance, if a business had $1 million in assets and offered 500,000 shares for sale, each share would be worth $2.00. This price is called the **initial value** or **par value**.

Prices = Points

All stock prices are listed in points. One point equals one dollar. If a stock is listed at 57 points, this means each share is worth $57.00. If you wanted to buy ten shares, you would pay $570.00. If you wanted to buy 300 shares, you would pay $17,100.00 (300 x 57).

Prices Go Up and Down

Once stocks are offered for sale on the stock market, their prices can rise or fall depending on what people are willing to pay. There are no rules on what price should be charged. If people think a company has great potential for making money, they will want to own stock in that company. All the people wanting to buy the stock create a demand that drives the price up. If only a few people want to buy the stock of the company, there is little demand for the stock and the company's stock prices may fall.

Many times the price of a company's stock is affected by conditions that have nothing to do with the performance of the business. Things that happen with the national economy or with the stock market in general can cause the company's stocks to rise or fall in price. The stock prices are determined not only by how well the company is doing, but also by how much confidence people have in the company's ability to make a profit and in the national economic picture.

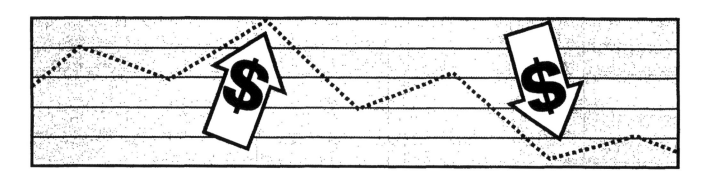

Example

Here are the stories of three companies that went public and what happened to their stock. All of the companies initially offered their stock at $5.00 per share.

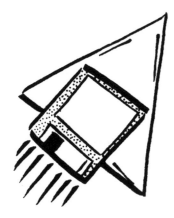

- **Company A** is a manufacturer of software for the Internet. Because its product had been reviewed favorably by several magazines and people who already used it were very happy with it, many people thought that this was a company whose sales would skyrocket once it had the money to do some intensive advertising. The company also arranged to have its software installed in computers manufactured by one of the largest computer companies. Therefore, the price of the stock skyrocketed. It was soon worth $10.00 per share, twice its initial offering price.

- **Company B** is a manufacturer of fertilizer that is used by corn farmers. The owners decided to sell stock in the company so they could raise the money to develop a new kind of fertilizer. Shortly after their stock was offered for sale, farmers in Iowa brought legal action against the company, saying that their fertilizer made the corn more susceptible to worms and that they had lost 40 percent of their crops to worms — more than in any previous year. The case had not gone to court, but the threat of a lawsuit scared off investors. No one wanted to own stock in a company that might go bankrupt. People who already owned the stock, sold their shares. The price of the stock fell to $1.20 per share.

- **Company C** is a business that provides temporary employees to other businesses. The owners decided to sell stock so they could expand and open offices in more locations. People saw this as a well-managed company that offered a needed service and the price for the stock quickly went up to $7.50 per share. However, two months after the initial stock offering, a report on national employment was released by the government. The report said that unemployment was higher than it had ever been in the last 20 years and that most companies did not plan on hiring any employees (temporary or permanent) to replace workers they had laid off. The economy was in a sad state of affairs and it was not expected that things would improve anytime in the near future. People who owned stock in Company C sold their stock in record numbers and the stock prices fell to $2.30 per share.

Figuring Prices

Name_____

Prices on the stock market are listed in points. One point equals one dollar. Changing from points to decimals is easy. Here are three examples.

    Company XYZ = 63 points = $63.00
    Company ABC = 75.43 points = $75.43
    Company CDE = 14.125 points = $14.125 (which may be rounded off
                                        to $14.13 in the newspapers).

To figure the price for buying or selling a stock, you multiply the number of shares by the price. Here are prices for the three companies listed above.

    100 shares of Company XYZ = 100 x $63.00 = $6,300.00
    200 shares of Company ABC = 200 x $75.43 = $15,086.00
    300 shares of Company CDE = 300 x $14.125 = $4,237.50

Find the price to buy the following stocks with the quantities and prices that are indicated.

1. 200 GnMotr at 56.75 = _____	8. 1000 USCan at 16.75 = _____
2. 100 Penny at 47.5 = _____	9. 800 SciGames at 26.625 = _____
3. 500 PepsiCo at 32.25 = _____	10. 400 WalMart at 23.875 = _____
4. 600 Safeway at 46.375 = _____	11. 250 Zenith at 10.25 = _____
5. 100 Disney at 75.125 = _____	12. 150 Gateway at 14.5 = _____
6. 300 BkNY at 26.875 = _____	13. 350 IBM at 26 = _____
7. 400 Allstate at 62.375 = _____	14. 850 NikeB at 63.125 = _____

15. If you had $100,00.00 with which to buy stocks, which of the stocks listed above would you choose?

_____

Prices and Events

Name _____

On the left is a listing of companies. On the right is a listing of events and newspaper headlines. For each event, tell which company would be affected and whether the effect would be positive (+) or negative (−).

Banana Computers - manufactures computers and software for personal and home use.

Global Communications - owns newspapers, magazines, radio and television stations.

Hip Hop - manufactures clothes, shoes and accessories for 12 to 18 year olds.

Biotec - manufactures a variety of mechanical devices to replace, repair or regulate human body parts.

ChocoBear - a chain of stores that sells chocolate and chocolate-related items.

SunCitrus - grows, harvests and processes citrus fruit.

1. Florida Reports the Best Crop of Oranges in 10 Years

   _____

2. Spending habits report shows that teenagers have more money to spend.

   _____

3. Patients who received the Biotec heart implants have threatened to sue to cover costs to correct design flaws

   _____

4. Study Claims Chocolate Prevents Tooth Decay

   _____

5. Banana's Revolutionary New Computer is a Fizzle

   _____

6. Global Communications wins 3 Pulitzer Prizes

   _____

7. Spending for food and personal products is up, but spending on entertainment and technology is down.

   _____

LOOK IT UP

Small Newspapers

Depending on what newspaper you refer to, the listing of stocks will give varying amounts of information. Papers that do not have a large business section may only list the name of the stock, the closing price, and the amount of increase or decrease over the previous day's closing price.

Example

company	close	change
Heinz	41	– .35
Mobil	131.625	+1.625

This says that Heinz closed at 41 points per share, which was .35 points lower than the closing price the day before. Likewise, Mobil closed at 131.625 points per share, up 1.625 points from the previous day's closing price.

Larger Newspapers

Other newspapers will give more complete information. In addition to the information shown above, they will list the dividends the company is paying, the high and low prices for the last 52 weeks, the price-earning ratio, the trading symbol, the number of shares traded in the day, and the high and low prices for the day. The following listings show more information than the brief listing above.

Example

| 52 week | | company | dividend | P/E | daily | | close | change |
high	low				high	low		
41.75	29.75	**Heinz**	2.8	23	41.75	40.0	41.625	+1.375
133.875	107.0	**Mobil**	3.3	19	133.0	126.875	129.25	–.875

In the first example Heinz's price varied between 29.75 and 41.75 during the last 52 weeks. During the day, the price varied from 40 to 41.75 points, finally closing at 41.625, which was 1.375 points more than it had closed at the day before. Heinz pays a yearly dividend of 2.8 points per share. The price/earning ratio is 23.

Mobil has varied between 107 and almost 134 points during the past year. While the day's price is nearly a point less than the day before, at some point during the day it was close to its yearly high.

Reading Stock Prices

Name _____

Look at the listings below that show the yearly and daily prices for several stocks. Then answer the questions that follow.

| 52 week | | company | daily | | | |
high	low		high	low	close	change
51.5	40.125	**ABC**	48.0	43.125	45.375	+ .375
107.0	90.25	**XYZ**	105.375	104.125	104.125	− .125
25.625	15.675	**PQR**	20.625	19.0	19.75	+ .5
67.5	58.5	**KLM**	64.375	60.875	64.75	+1.0
12.75	6.625	**STU**	10.5	9.25	9.5	− .25

1. What was PQR's closing price? _____

2. Which stock closed 1 point higher than yesterday? _____

3. Which stocks went up in price from yesterday's price? _____
   Which stocks went down? _____

4. Which stock had a closing price that was the same as its daily low? _____

5. What is the cheapest you could have bought KLM stock for this last year? _____

6. What is the most you could have paid for XYZ stock today? _____

7. What was XYZ's highest price during the last year? _____
   How much higher was that price than its lowest yearly price? _____

8. What was the closing price of ABC stock yesterday? _____

9. What was the closing price of XYZ stock yesterday? _____

10. What stock had the greatest daily price variation? _____

11. What stock had the smallest price variation during the last 52 weeks? _____

Making Money with Stocks

The people who buy stock in a business become joint owners and share in the assets and income of the company. People buy stocks because they want to invest their money; that is, they want to make money with their money.

Sock, Bank or Stocks?

If you put your money in a sock and stick it under the bed, after two years you will have exactly the same amount as you started with. If you put the money in a bank in a savings account, you will earn interest (usually about 5%) on your money and will have slightly more money at the end of two years than when you began.

The other thing you could do with the money is buy stocks. While this form of investment is more risky (meaning you could lose money as well as make money) than keeping the money under the bed or putting it in a federally-insured bank, you have the possibility of making more money. This is why investing in the stock market is called **speculative** — there are no guarantees that you will make money or if you do make money, how much you will make.

Over time stocks have made more money for people than other forms of

investment. Between 1926 and 1993 common stocks increased an average of 10% per year, bonds increased 5%, and U.S. Treasury bills went up 3.7%. If you had invested one dollar in the stock market in 1926, that investment would be worth $800 in 1993. That's a fair return on your investment. But remember, there are no guarantees with stocks. Any particular stock you choose could go down as well as up. If the company goes bankrupt, you could lose all the money you put into it.

How to Make Money with Stocks

People make money from their stock ownership by getting dividends (usually paid quarterly) and by selling the stock when it goes up in price. Dividends are a share of the profits that are usually paid every quarter. A company can, however, choose not to distribute the profits if the board of directors feels that it needs to keep the money in the business for some reason.

The other way that people make money by owning stocks is to sell the stock when the price is higher than what it was when they bought the stock. If you own 100 shares in a company that you bought for

$2.00 per share and the stock price goes up to $5.00 per share, you will make a profit of $3.00 per share when you sell it. If you sold all 100 shares, you would make $300.00. The famous saying for making money in this way is, **"Buy Low, Sell High."**

The other piece of advice that people who are investing in the stock market often get is to be prepared to hold onto their stocks for a long period of time. A company's stock prices will usually change slowly over a long period of time. It is not usual for the price of a stock to change rapidly, either up or down. An example of how you can make money by buying stock and holding on to it for a period of time is McDonald's stock. If you had bought 10 shares of stock in 1965 for $22.50 each, by 1993 the stock would have split ten times and your stocks would be worth about $96,000.

Example

Joey buys 100 shares of ABC company for $5.00 per share, for a total price of $500.00. He owns the stock for one year. During that time the company has made a profit and has paid its stockholders $.50 per share each quarter (or $50 for the 100 shares).

At the end of the year the stock is now worth $7.50 per share. Joey decides to sell the stock. He gets $750.00 for his 100 shares. His total profit would look like this:

dividends	$50.00 (1st quarter)
	$50.00 (2nd quarter)
	$50.00 (3rd quarter)
	$50.00 (4th quarter)
sale of stock	$750.00
total income	$950.00
less original cost	−$500.00
total profit	**$450.00**

The money that Joey makes from selling the stock is called a **capital gain**.

Making Money with Stocks

Name_____

For each of the following situations, find out how much money each person made or lost.

1. Doug Out was a baseball fan, so he invested in Sport Shoe, a company that manufactures various kinds of sports shoes and protective gear. He bought 200 shares at 23.25. Two years later, he sold all 200 shares at 20.125. He didn't receive any dividends.

   initial investment   (200 x 23.25) = _____
   sale   (200 x 20.125) = _____
   profit or loss   _____

2. Sadie Hogcaller loved country music, so she invested in MusicWest, a company that produces country music disks, concert tours, and television shows. She bought 400 shares at 27.125. During the two years she had the stock, she received 8 dividends of .25 per share. She sold the stock at 33.25.

   initial investment   _____
   dividends   _____
   sale price   _____
   profit or loss   _____

3. Helga Healthwise will only eat organic food and only invests in companies that promote practices that are healthy for people and the environment. She bought 100 shares of Organicare at 6.75. She held the stock for 3 years and sold the stock at 12.625. During that time she received 12 dividends of $.50 per share.

   initial investment   _____
   dividends   _____
   sale price   _____
   profit or loss   _____

Buy or Sell?

Name _____

The following chart shows the prices of several stocks over a period of time. Remembering the advice, "buy low; sell high," tell when you would buy each stock, when you would sell the stock and what profit you would make on each stock.

	6/15/95	7/20/96	9/3/96	11/12/96	1/31/97	3/17/97	6/4/97	10/3/97
Stock A	17.25	15.125	15.75	16.625	17.0	16.875	19.375	24.625
Stock B	12.0	12.375	11.875	11.5	10.5	11.625	12.625	12.5
Stock C	52.125	53.0	50.125	53.25	55.75	57.625	56.375	56.0
Stock D	33.375	35.625	37.125	39.125	38.875	38.625	39.0	36.75
Stock E	48.0	47.125	46.75	45.875	46.125	50.875	51.375	51.125
Stock F	5.675	6.125	7.75	5.875	6.375	8.375	9.875	10.75

	Buy	**Sell**	**Profit per share**	**Profit per 100 shares**
Stock A				
Stock B				
Stock C				
Stock D				
Stock E				
Stock F				

Charting Prices

Name_____

Choose a stock whose price is reported regularly in your newspaper. Make a graph that shows the closing price every day for 2 weeks.

Graph of_____ (company) for the weeks of_____

Mon.	Tues.	Wed.	Thurs.	Fri.	Mon.	Tues.	Wed.	Thurs.	Fri.

Stock Exchanges

What is an Exchange?

A stock exchange is a place where people who want to buy and sell stocks get together. Almost every country has its own stock exchange. There are nine stock exchanges in the United States: two main exchanges and seven regional exchanges. In addition to the exchanges, which are actual places, there is the NASDAQ, which is not a place but a network of computers that allows stock brokers to buy and sell stocks that are listed in this system.

Stock Exchanges

The New York Stock Exchange is the largest stock market in the United States. It is located in New York City. It was founded in 1792 by 24 men, and the exchange has operated almost without interruption since that time. Stocks can be listed on both the New York Stock Exchange and on regional exchanges.

The American Stock Exchange is the second largest in the country and is also located in New York City. It was founded in 1849. It has fewer members and trades fewer stocks.

Regional exchanges provide a market for many local or regional stocks that do not meet the requirements to be listed on the New York or American Exchange. They may also list some stocks that are listed on the major exchanges.

Over-the-Counter

Of the more that 20,000 securities that are traded, only about 3,000 are listed on any exchange. These stocks are said to be "listed." The rest are traded "over-the-counter" (OTC) and are said to be "unlisted." There is no central marketplace for these stocks. They are traded through a network of computers. The prices for only the most widely traded OTC stocks will appear in the newspaper. The National Association of Securities Dealers Automatic Quotations (NASDAQ) provides information on the larger, better-known over-the-counter stocks, but not all the OTC stocks. The price of the largest NASDAQ stocks are listed in the newspaper.

Which Exchange?

Name_____

Look at these stock names and find them in the newspaper. Tell which exchange they are listed on and what the closing price was.

Stock	NYSE	AMEX	NASDAQ	Closing price	Date
Costco					
Xerox					
Lincare					
American Airlines					
Nike					
Macromedia					
Wendy's					
Applebee's					
Intel					

Add two stocks for each exchange, listing the company name and the closing price.

New York Stock Exchange

_____

_____

NASDAQ

_____

_____

American Stock Exchange

_____

_____

BENCHMARKS

Several indexes have been developed that measure the ups and downs of specific stocks and the stock market in general. By referring to these indexes, you can tell whether your stock is doing as well as other stocks. If the market in general is going up and your stock is going down, it would indicate that your stock is not doing well. If, however, the average price of stocks on the stock market have gone up 10 percent during a year and your stock has gone up 20 percent, then you have picked a winner. Comparing the stocks in your portfolio to these indexes will allow you to better judge whether your stock is performing well or not.

Dow Jones Industrial Average

The **Dow Jones Industrial Average** is a measure of market prices that is based on 30 leading companies on the New York Stock Exchange. The DJIA was first calculated by Charles Dow in 1884. He took the average of 11 stocks. Over the years it is has reflected the general trend of the stock market. In 1900 the Dow was a little less than 100, and in 1998 it passed the 9000 mark. Usually the index fluctuates slowly up and down, but some events, like the great national depression of 1931 and 1932, have caused the index to fall dramatically.

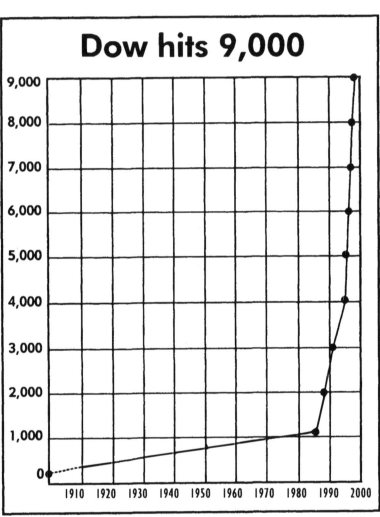

S & P 500

The most widely followed measure of the health of the stock market after the Dow is the **Standard and Poor's 500**. The Standard and Poor's 500 (S & P 500) is an average of 500 major stocks. Because it includes prices on more stocks than the Dow Jones index, it is more representative of the stock market in general. That is, if the stock market is going up, the S & P 500 will also be going up. If the stock market is falling, the S & P 500 will most accurately reflect this fall. The index is composed mostly of stocks on the New York Stock Exchange but does include some stocks on the American Exchange and some over-the-counter stocks.

Other Indexes

The **NYSE Composite Index** reflects the overall price changes of all common stocks listed on the New York Stock Exchange. The index compares the average stock prices to the average price on December 31, 1965, when the average was 50. This means that if the composite index is 300, the average price is six times what the average price was when the index originated in 1965.

The American Stock Exchange has an index called the **American Stock Exchange Market (AMEX) Index** that measures performance of 800 stocks on the American Exchange. Likewise, the NASDAQ has an index of over-the-counter stocks. It is the **OTC (Over-the-Counter) Index**. It covers over 5000 over-the-counter stocks.

If you are investing money in the stock market, you should be aware of these indexes and whether they are moving up or down, just as you should follow the stocks you own. You can find these indexes printed in the newspaper along with the stock quotes.

MARKET REPORT

Index	% chg
Dow Jones	+14
AMEX	+2
S & P 500	−5
N Y S E	−8
NASDAQ	+10

Silva Portfolio +9

Jones Portfolio −10

Something To Do

Index Watching

- *Choose one of the indexes (Dow Jones, S & P 500, or NASDAQ) and graph the index for a week or more.*
- *Also choose a company that you think would be a good investment. Make another graph of this stock over the same period of time.*

Stockbrokers and Commissions

Role of the Stockbroker

A stockbroker is a person who buys and sells stocks for people who want to invest in securities. This person is licensed to buy and sell stocks and charges a commission each time stocks are bought or sold. Historically, if you wanted to buy stock, you would visit a stockbroker (a real person) at a stock brokerage (an office or building). Since the advent of computers and the Internet, many stock transactions can be made using computers and telephones.

Commission

Whether you deal with the stockbroker in person or over the telephone or computer, you will still have to pay a commission. A commission is the money you pay the stockbroker for buying or selling the stock for you. It is a percentage of the total sale. Depending on how much advice and service you receive, you will pay a different commission. Stockbrokers who don't give you advice (they only buy and sell as you tell them to) are called discount brokers and charge a smaller percentage as a commission.

Figuring Commission

To figure commission, you change the commission (expressed as a percentage) to a decimal and multiply that times the value of the total sale or purchase.

Example:

5% commission on $1,000
.05 x $1,000.00 = $50.00

3% commission on $5,000
.03 x $5,000.00 = $150.00

4% commission on 200 shares at 28.125 per share
.04 x (200 x 28.125) = .04 x 5,625.00 = $225.00

Example:

George bought 1,000 shares of Good Time Movie Company for $5.00 per share. His broker charged him a 3% commission.

The sale was for $5,000.00 (1000 x $5.00)
The commission was 3% of $5,000.00
.03 x 5,000.00 = $150.00

Buying Stocks

This is what happens when you go to a stockbroker to buy stock.

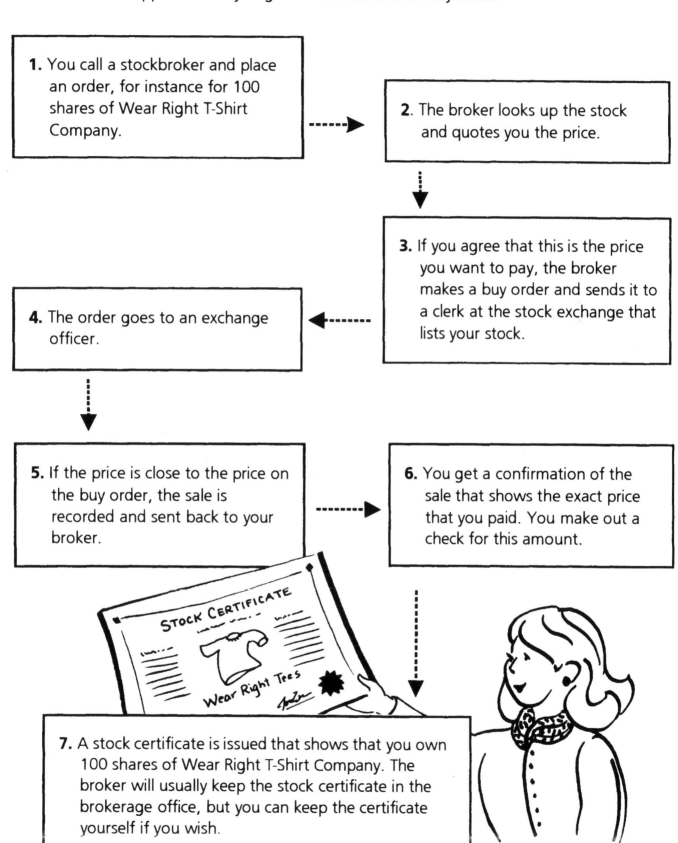

1. You call a stockbroker and place an order, for instance for 100 shares of Wear Right T-Shirt Company.

2. The broker looks up the stock and quotes you the price.

3. If you agree that this is the price you want to pay, the broker makes a buy order and sends it to a clerk at the stock exchange that lists your stock.

4. The order goes to an exchange officer.

5. If the price is close to the price on the buy order, the sale is recorded and sent back to your broker.

6. You get a confirmation of the sale that shows the exact price that you paid. You make out a check for this amount.

7. A stock certificate is issued that shows that you own 100 shares of Wear Right T-Shirt Company. The broker will usually keep the stock certificate in the brokerage office, but you can keep the certificate yourself if you wish.

Figuring Commission

Name _____

Figure the commission of these purchases and sales of stock.

1. John buys 400 shares of General Motors at 59.25. His broker charges him a 3% commission.

2. Joslyn sells 500 shares of Safeway at 48. She pays her broker a 4% commission.

3. Irma buys 100 shares of AT&T at 39.625 and 100 shares of Mattel at 26.375. She is charged a 5% commission.

4. Jack N. Bock sells 200 shares of McDonald's at 46.5 and buys 100 shares of Harley Davidson at 41.5. He is charged a 4% commission on each transaction.

5. Nick sells 500 shares of America Online at 37.75 and pays a commission of 3%.

6. Heather sells 500 shares of Boeing at 109.125 and buys 300 shares of DuPont at 112.25 and 100 shares of Gap at 33.375. She pays a 5% commission.

Buying Stock

Name_____

Refer to a current listing of stock prices. Choose five stocks that you think would be good investments. Record the name and price for each stock and then convert the price to dollars and figure how much you would have to pay to buy 200 shares and pay your stockbroker a 3 percent commission.

1. Stock _____   price _____ (in points)
    200 shares at $_____ per share = a purchase price of $_____
    3% commission = _____
    Total price (purchase price + commission) = _____

2. Stock _____   price _____ (in points)
    200 shares at $_____ per share = a purchase price of $_____
    3% commission = _____
    Total price (purchase price + commission) = _____

3. Stock _____   price _____ (in points)
    200 shares at $_____ per share = a purchase price of $_____
    3% commission = _____
    Total price (purchase price + commission) = _____

4. Stock _____   price _____ (in points)
    200 shares at $_____ per share = a purchase price of $_____
    3% commission = _____
    Total price (purchase price + commission) = _____

5. Stock _____   price _____ (in points)
    200 shares at $_____ per share = a purchase price of $_____
    3% commission = _____
    Total price (purchase price + commission) = _____

How to Pick a Winner

You make money on the stock market when stocks you have bought go up in price and you are able to sell them at a higher price than the price you paid to purchase them. The better you are at noticing companies that supply products or services that people need or at predicting trends, the better you will be in picking stocks that will increase in price. Remember that it is just as easy to lose money on the stock market as it is to make money. If you do not do your homework, you may choose stocks that will not increase in price.

Here are some tips for finding stocks that will be sound, money-making purchases:

- *Keep your eyes open for new businesses that are meeting a need that other companies have not met.*

- *Look for problems with other competing companies. If a competitor's business is not doing well, it may mean that the company you have invested in will pick up business that the competitor has lost.*

- *Read the newspaper and listen to the news. Think about how the news will affect the price of the stocks.*

- *Diversify. That is, buy stocks in different fields of the economy.*

- *Know something about the company and the products or services it provides. Ask, "What is the future for this company's products?"*

- *Look for companies whose stocks are reasonably priced.*

- *Weigh your risk versus your profit. A company that is very risky might go up in price a lot, but it also might go down. Decide if you are willing to take that chance.*

- *Try to choose companies that will make gradual increases over time rather than making quick rises.*

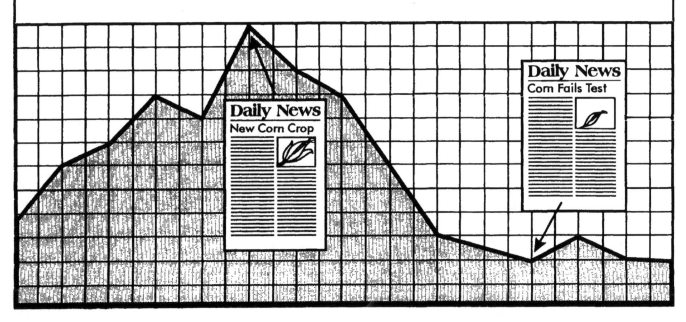

The Right Choice

Name_____

Read the tips on selecting a good stock and then select a company whose stock is listed on one of the exchanges or the NASDAQ. Explain why you think this would be a good stock to own. Describe the company, what products or services it offers. Tell why you think it is better than its competitors and why it would be a wise investment.

My stock pick is _____ .

_____
_____
_____
_____
_____
_____
_____
_____
_____
_____
_____
_____
_____
_____

Stock Market Game
Short Version

Overview

When you follow stock prices of real companies on the stock market, the prices will change very little from day to day. For this reason, it is hard for students to see how prices vary and to make a profit or loss with their stock purchases unless they are allowed to follow the market for at least several months. This short version of the Stock Market Game is intended to be used when it is not possible to allocate a long period of time to follow stocks on the stock market, or to be used as a short introduction to trading and how news and market forces affect stock prices. This shorter version of the game provides students with the opportunity to invest in hypothetical companies. Each day students are provided with news releases and price changes. They can, therefore, quickly see the prices of their selected stocks go up or down and make the appropriate decisions about buying and selling.

This simulation will take about a week of class time. You will give students a list of stocks from which they will chose a portfolio. You will then issue the news reports at the appropriate intervals. Based on the news reports, students may chose to buy, sell, or keep their stocks. You will also announce the stock prices each day. The stock prices will fluctuate each day much more than stock prices would normally fluctuate during a day of trading, but this will allow students to see greater gains or losses in their stocks in a short amount of time. The prices will often reflect news about the company that was previously announced through the news reports. This gives students an opportunity to judge how current events affect the stocks' prices. As a result of spending a week of buying and selling these imaginary stocks, students should gain a good understanding of how to gauge the ups and downs of the market and their particular stocks. After this experi-

ence, you may choose to do the longer stock market simulation that allows them to invest in real stocks.

Throughout the simulation, remind students that stock prices are partially determined by concrete factors like profits, losses, and assets, but they are also influenced by the emotions of the stockholders and the psychology of the market as a whole. If people think a company will lose money, that fear may be enough to cause the prices to plummet even though the company is on sound financial ground. If a company is a sound company and you have reason to believe that the dip in price is temporary and due mostly to buyers' fears, then it is a good time to buy that stock and wait for the stock to go up.

Procedure

Day 1

1. Duplicate and pass out the company profiles. Go through each company profile and discuss the products or services it offers. Explain to students that they will be making their stock purchases from these companies. After they choose their initial purchases, they will be given a chance each day to buy or sell stocks.

2. Review how to figure purchase or sale price (stock price x number of shares) and commission (total price x commission rate).

3. Give students copies of the Trading Record, Portfolio Record, and Cash Reserve sheets. These sheets are used to keep track of the stocks that they buy and sell and the money they have in their reserve accounts. Go through an example together, showing students how to record purchases and sales and how to transfer them to their stock

portfolios and cash reserve sheets. See examples on pages 61 to 63.

4. Review rules of the simulation with students. The rules are:

- They have $50,000 with which to purchase stock.
- They have to own at least two different stocks.
- They cannot own more than 500 shares of any one stock.
- They have to buy and sell in multiples of 100.
- They must sell at least 100 shares and buy 100 shares of a new stock each trading period.
- They must pay a commission of 3% on all stock purchases and sales.
- Money that is not invested in stocks will be held in a cash reserve account. When stocks are sold, the money from the sales goes into the cash reserve account. They can never spend more money than they have in the cash account to buy new stocks.

5. While it is not a rule of the game, encourage students to limit their stock choices to no more than five stocks. If they own more than five stocks, it becomes difficult for them to follow the stocks and keep track of the money transactions.

6. Post the beginning prices for the stocks.

7. Have students select their stocks and record them on their Trading Record and Stock Portfolio sheets. They may not spend more than $50,000. Money that they have left over after purchasing stocks will be recorded on their Cash Reserve sheet. They will keep a continuing record of their cash reserve on this record sheets. For complete instructions on recording transactions, see page 52. For examples showing how to record information on the various records sheets, see pages 61 to 63.

8. Read the first news report.

Day 2

1. Read the early edition news report.

2. Post the daily stock prices.

3. Give students time to decide which stocks they want to buy and sell. Have them record their sales and purchases on their Trading Records and then transfer the information to the Stock Portfolio. Any changes in their cash reserves should be recorded on the Cash Reserve record sheets.

4. Collect record sheets.

5. Read the late edition news report.

Day 3

1. Read the early edition news report.

2. Post the daily stock prices.

3. Give students time to decide which stocks they want to buy and sell. Have them record their sales and purchases on their Trading Records and then transfer the information to the Stock Portfolio. Any changes in their cash reserves should be recorded on the Cash Reserve record sheets.

4. Collect record sheets.

5. Read the late edition news report.

Day 4

1. Read the early edition news report.

2. Post the daily stock prices.

3. Give students time to decide which stocks they want to buy and sell. Have them record their sales and purchases on their Trading Records and then transfer the information to the Stock Portfolio. Any changes in their cash reserves should be recorded on the Cash Reserve record sheets.

4. Collect all record sheets.

5. Read the late edition news report.

Day 5

1. Post the daily stock prices.

2. Have students record the final value of their portfolios, add the money they have in their cash reserve, and figure the amount of money they made during the week.

3. Collect all record sheets.

Rules

- You have $50,000 with which to purchase stocks.

- You have to own at least two different stocks.

- You cannot own more than 500 shares of any one stock.

- You have to buy and sell in multiples of 100.

- You must sell at least 100 shares each day.

- You must buy at least 100 shares of a new stock each day.

- You have to pay a commission of 3% on all stock purchases and sales.

- Money that is not invested in stocks will be held in a cash reserve account. When stocks are sold, the money from the sales goes into your cash reserve account. You can never spend more money than you have in the cash account to buy new stocks.

Company Profiles

Cool Shoes

Cool Shoes produces casual shoes and athletic shoes for the younger customer. It has a line of 25 styles and each year brings out a new style it names after a famous athlete. The stock has been traded publicly for four years, and during that time the price has gone from 4.5 to over 25. The company continues to add new products and production facilities. It currently owns two manufacturing plants and subcontracts some of its manufacturing to other companies. It advertises nationally in magazines and television. The company donates a portion of its profits to organizations that sponsor athletics for elementary through high school students and that provide education and counseling to keep young people off drugs.

Specific Foods

Specific Foods' motto is "Foods for the Future." The company makes a line of foods that contain soybeans, seaweed, and plankton. These are sources of protein that Specific Foods claims will be readily available in the future and do not take large amounts of expensive land to grow. The company's foods are sold mainly through health food stores and by mail order, but there is a growing market in developing nations and Asian countries. Specific Foods has a world-wide distribution system and sales have grown tenfold in the last five years. The stock has been traded on the stock market for two years.

J. P. Nickel

This old retail establishment has been in business since 1904. By 1985 the company had a store in every city with a population of 30,000 or more and a profitable catalog order business. Since 1985 the company has closed many of its stores in city centers, claiming that real estate costs and the movement of businesses to malls made it unprofitable to keep these stores open. It now operates stores in 850 shopping malls and has continued with catalog outlets in another 600 locations. When J. P. Nickel moved to the malls, it dropped home improvement and hardware products but kept clothing, jewelry, housewares, and home entertainment. Most of these products are priced for middle-income families. Since this change in location and marketing, profits have improved.

BEST BEACH WEAR

This young company produces a line of clothing, shoes, and accessories for beach-goers. It has recently branched out and makes a line of suntan products and a line of clothing for snowboarders. The company was started by two surfers in Malibu, California. They knew what young beach-goers liked to wear, and they were able to capitalize on their youthful attitudes and their sense of design. The company went public three years ago and the founders left the day-to-day managing of the company to other people while they have returned to their first love, surfing. Best Beach Wear is expensive, but the quality has always been good. Sales skyrocket in the summer but usually fall off during the winter. The owners are hoping that their new line of clothing for snowboarders will help them even out yearly sales.

Mrs. Gooey's Cookies and Candies

This company was started by Mrs. Morton in 1855, when she sold her homemade baked goods, candies, and preserves to neighbors. The company makes a large variety of baked goods (cookies, breads, cakes, pies) as well as candies, jams, jellies, barbecue sauce, snack bars, and flavored popcorn. While most of these products are sold in grocery stores, some of the products are sold in vending machines, and the highest quality candies are sold in Mrs. Gooey's candy shops that are typically located in shopping malls. Mrs. Gooey's also supplies restaurants, hospitals, airlines, college dining facilities, and the military with baked goods, jams and jellies.

ALTERNATE POWER COMPANY

Alternate Power is a company that produces electricity through the use of solar and wind power. It started in 1960 as a small group of friends who wanted to do something good for the environment. They used solar panels to produce enough energy for their own use. Over the years the company grew and added wind power as an energy source. It is now the biggest producer of alternate energy. It has 36 power-generating plants in 12 countries. The company plans on opening 12 more power plants in the next five years. The energy that is produced by the company is usually sold to larger electric utilities. Once the facilities are in place, expenses are much less than other electricity-producing facilities, so it is a very profitable company. The stock has been traded publicly for eight years.

First Farms

First Farms is a large farming corporation that raises a number of crops, but specializes in wheat, corn, tomatoes, lettuce, peanuts, sugar, rice, tobacco, and cotton. The company has a wide distribution system and is able to sell at competitive prices. It has gone through a period of rapid expansion, buying up land; therefore, it pays a large portion of its profits to cover interest on its loans. First Farms, however, is as good at marketing its products as it is at growing them, so sales have increased steadily. The company has recently expanded into processing (milling and refining the products it raises) and has a small bio-engineering company that is using genetics to produce better, more disease-resistant types of some crops.

I Can Computers

This is a new computer company that claims its computers and software are so simple to operate that both young children and older people, who grew up before the computer age, can easily use the machines. The cost of buying one of these systems is relatively cheap. The company's market is homes and early grades in schools. It hopes to put one of these computers in every home and in each kindergarten through third-grade classroom. The company has been on the stock market for only one year. Its motto is, "Buy an I Can Computer and You Can." Profits from sales in North America have doubled every six months, and the company has plans to market the computers in several other countries.

CHEAP FUEL

Cheap Fuel is a chain of gas stations that sells gasoline and oil at prices that are cheaper than their competition's. It has stations in every city with a population more than 10,000, and the company has plans to expand worldwide. It buys crude oil from other producers and then refines it, so it does not have the exploration expenses of some oil companies. Cheap Fuel stations have automated the process of purchasing fuel so that customers can get in and out fast, it has employees who clean customers' windows and check their oil, and its products are less expensive than the competition's. Cheap Fuel is a popular choice for people who want to save money, who want a little extra service, or who are in a hurry. The company's motto is, "A Little Extra Service Without the Extra Price."

Phase Pharmaceuticals

Phase is one of the oldest and most established companies involved in developing and marketing medications and health products around the world. It has a good record of thorough testing of its products before they are introduced into the marketplace, so it has had very few lawsuits. It produces medications for a variety of physical ailments and the company is constantly working on new cures. While sales are large, Phase Pharmaceuticals also has large expenses for developing new products and obtaining hard-to-get ingredients. Phase used to manufacture a line of health care products like bandages, soaps, and over-the-counter products but recently sold off that part of the business. The company found that the health care portion of their business was not as profitable as prescription drugs. By selling off that line of products, it decreased its sales, but increased profits by 3%.

Whiz Entertainment

Whiz Entertainment was formed by consolidating several smaller companies, all of which specialized in entertaining young people. The company now owns Wonder Comics, Young Heart Production Company (producer of G-rated movies), Beegate Productions (producer of television programs for 2- through 12-year-olds), Whiz Video, Rebus Records, and Silver Lining Books. Whiz prides itself on providing programs, music, videos and books that are educational as well as entertaining. It has won awards from a large number of groups concerned with the quality of children's entertainment. It has successfully turned two of its comic series into cartoons. In addition to income from movie receipts and sales of its other products, the company has successfully licensed products based on its comic, television and movie characters. This arrangement has allowed it to increase its income without having to invest additional money or time for development or advertising.

Stock Prices

The following are the stock prices that you will use to update students on the status of their stocks each day. When the simulation begins, give them the opening prices for all stocks before they decide which stocks they will buy. At the beginning of each day, post the stock prices for that day.

Do not duplicate this page or give it to students.

	Day 1	Day 2	Day 3	Day 4	Day 5
Alternate Power	28.25	18.125	27.5	29	32.75
Best Beach Wear	11	13.25	16.5	18	10.125
Cheap Fuel	15.625	12.5	11	15.25	16.75
Cool Shoes	25.25	27.625	29	25	31.5
First Farms	37.874	29.125	32	34.75	38.75
I Can Computers	7.375	10.25	15.625	10.5	14.5
J. P. Nickel	48.25	54.5	57	58.125	53.5
Mrs. Gooey's	43.75	40.5	43.25	47.125	50.75
Phase Pharmaceuticals	60.125	64.125	74.25	75.5	73.125
Specific Foods	8.5	10.5	13.125	17.375	16.875
Whiz Entertainment	20.75	20	25.125	28	29.5

Stock Prices

Alternate Power	28.25	+ .5	J. P. Nickel	48.25	+2.125
Best Beach Wear	11	– .375	Mrs. Gooey's	43.75	+ .875
Cheap Fuel	15.625	+ 1.75	Phase Pharmaceuticals	60.125	+1.875
Cool Shoes	25.125	– .25	Specific Foods	8.5	– .625
First Farms	37.875	+ 1.125	Whiz Entertainment	20.75	+ .125
I Can Computers	7.375	– .625			

Companies in the News

NEW YORK - J. P. Nickel has announced plans to open another five stores in Texas, Arizona and California. A company spokesperson said that above-average sales in existing outlets has allowed the company to open these new stores in cities that are experiencing rapid population growth.

BOSTON - The American Medical Association is recommending that people limit their consumption of candy and sweets. The Association says that on the average, people are 30 pounds overweight and this single change in eating habits could help to solve the problem.

NEW YORK - The Dow Jones Industrial Average was up 3 points.

SAN FRANCISCO - Pacific Electric announced that it will no longer build nuclear or coal-burning power plants. All future electric power generation will be done with ecological power sources like wind and solar. As the largest producer of power in the West, its decision will undoubtedly affect electric prices.

ATLANTA - The National Advertisers Association at its annual conference drafted a resolution stating that all members will refrain from creating ads for tobacco products that are targeted toward young people.

The Stock Market News

Companies in the News

MALIBU - After a six-month leave of absence from managing Best Beach Wear, the company's owners have decided to come back to the company they started and take a more active part in the day-to-day workings of the business. They cite boredom with the leisure life and a need to correct errors that were made in their absence as the reasons for their return.

KANSAS CITY - Prices for corn are 10% higher this year than they were last year, but rice farmers fear that they will see a decline in their crop's prices due to large rice crops in other parts of the world. A failed wheat crop in Russia promises to provide a good market for wheat farmers.

LOS ANGELES - Travelers this summer will find higher prices at the pumps due to trade embargoes imposed by our country against six oil-producing countries. This move comes as a retaliation for the oil-producing countries' unwillingness to lift import taxes on farm products produced in this country.

SANTA CLARA - Orange computers, the largest manufacturer of personal computers, announced a second-quarter loss of 4 million dollars.

NEW YORK - The Dow Jones rose again today. It is up 2.25 points.

Stock Prices

Alternate Power	_____	J. P. Nickel	_____
Best Beach Wear	_____	Mrs. Gooey's	_____
Cheap Fuel	_____	Phase Pharmaceuticals	_____
Cool Shoes	_____	Specific Foods	_____
First Farms	_____	Whiz Entertainment	_____
I Can Computers	_____		

Companies in the News

LOS ANGELES - Among the Oscar nominations for best documentary this year is "Eager Young Hero," the story of how a young girl's determination allowed her to overcome physical limitations and help other people. The movie was produced by Young Heart Productions.

WASHINGTON - The National Food and Drug Administration has approved Phase Pharmaceuticals' new weight control medication. The medication is available only with a prescription, but tests show the drug to be effective 80% of the time.

NEW YORK - As stock prices continue to rise (up another 4 points today), the Federal Reserve Board is talking about raising interest rates by one half to one percent to offset the bull market. Commission chairperson Richard Rich said the commission will meet next week.

DALLAS - Cool Shoes announced that it is bringing out a whole line of comfortable walking shoes for older people. The Texas company has plans to expand its market and capture some of the spending power of retired citizens.

SAN FRANCISCO - The American Dietitians' Association has announced the results of a three-year study that supports evidence that eating soy products prevents or reduces the chances of getting four kinds of cancers. Specific Foods has taken this opportunity to offer customers free information about soybean products and recipes on their website.

The Stock Market News

Companies in the News

WASHINGTON - As a part of the newly adopted budget, the government is setting aside 5 million dollars for technology education. The major portion of this money will be allocated to schools to buy computers and software for elementary students.

ATLANTA - Remarkable Cards has announced an advertising alliance between the nation's largest card company and the nation's largest candy company, Mrs. Gooey's. The two companies will combine their advertising dollars to promote cards and candies for major holidays like Valentine's Day, Mother's Day and Easter.

OMAHA - Pork producers are predicting a record year in pork consumption as a result of an intensive advertising campaign. Corn and soybean producers are also rejoicing at this news, since corn and soybeans are the major food sources for pigs.

LOS ANGELES - Whiz Entertainment has been sued by a cooperative of private advertising firms who say that its practice of advertising its own products on Beegate shows puts the advertising firms and their clients at an unfair disadvantage.

WASHINGTON - In anticipation of a rise in interest rates, the market closed down 10 points. The Federal Reserve Board's decision to postpone its meeting for another week will mean that the market will be unstable until a decision about interest rates is made.

Stock Prices

Alternate Power	_____	J. P. Nickel	_____
Best Beach Wear	_____	Mrs. Gooey's	_____
Cheap Fuel	_____	Phase Pharmaceuticals	_____
Cool Shoes	_____	Specific Foods	_____
First Farms	_____	Whiz Entertainment	_____
I Can Computers	_____		

Companies in the News

SAN FRANCISCO - Banana Computers has offered to buy out I Can Computers, a move that would make it the largest producer of low-cost, home-use computers. Details of the buy-out offer were not available.

MIAMI - Cool Shoes has lost a bid to be the supplier of athletic shoes for the National Foot Games.

NEW YORK - Retail sales reached a record during the last quarter. Major retailers posted the largest profits in the past 15 years. The majority of sales increases came from sales to middle-income families for clothing and entertainment.

NEW YORK - The stock market rallied today, closing 4.375 points ahead of yesterday's closing.

CINCINNATI - The World Good Health Organization, meeting in this city for a biannual conference, passed a resolution to encourage citizens in Third World countries to eat soybean and lentil products. Increased consumption of these products could improve health in nations where large numbers of people consume less that the daily recommended levels of nourishment.

LONDON - The British division of Phase Pharmaceuticals has acquired the European license to manufacture and distribute a new type of allergy medication that is more effective in smaller dosages than current allergy drugs. The company hopes to license the drug in this country before the end of the year.

The Stock Market News

Companies in the News

AMSTERDAM - Alternate Power just opened a new power-generating facility that will supply power to this city. The power plant uses tidal action to generate electricity. Construction ran $4 million over the original budget, so the company does not anticipate a profit from this facility for many years.

DENVER - Mrs. Gooey's Cookies and Candies has announced an agreement with Specific Foods to develop baked goods using soybeans. These new baked goods will be sold as low-fat, healthy alternatives to Mrs. Gooey's typical products. The company feels that it should be able to capture a growing market of health-conscious people who are not willing to give up desserts.

NEW YORK - Yesterday's short increase in prices was reversed with prices closing down 2.75 points today.

DETROIT - All major car manufacturers have announced plans to produce cars next year that will get 30% better gas mileage.

CHICAGO - Cheap Fuel just won the Traveler's Club award for good service and value. The club chooses only three recipients each year, and this is the fourth time Cheap Fuels has won this honor.

SANTA CLARA - Can Do Software has filed a suit against I Can Computers alleging that I Can stole its software and incorporated it into its newest computers. I Can Computers claims that all its software was developed by its own design engineers. The lawsuit could take a year to resolve and will cost both firms hundreds of thousands of dollars in court costs.

Stock Prices

Alternate Power	_____	J. P. Nickel	_____
Best Beach Wear	_____	Mrs. Gooey's	_____
Cheap Fuel	_____	Phase Pharmaceuticals	_____
Cool Shoes	_____	Specific Foods	_____
First Farms	_____	Whiz Entertainment	_____
I Can Computers	_____		

Companies in the News

CHICAGO - First Farms has announced an agreement to buy out Specific Foods. The consolidation allows First Farms to continue to expand into new markets. The offer gives Specific Foods stockholders a stock price that is 3 points higher than the current price.

MALIBU - Best Beach Wear's quarterly report shows that sales of its new line of snow apparel did not do as well as anticipated. The company lost 2 million dollars. It says it will continue to produce winter clothing while concentrating on building its line of summer apparel.

LITTLE ROCK - MallMart, a chain of discount stores will build 100 new stores in shopping malls around the nation. These upscale versions of the discount chain's typical retail center will be in direct competition with J. P. Nickel, one of the nation's oldest retailers

LAS VEGAS - Whiz Entertainment will open a major entertainment center for young people. The center will rival current Las Vegas attractions in terms of size and glitz but will offer quality entertainment for 3 through 12-year-olds.

BOSTON - Cool Shoes will be a major sponsor of the Boston Marathon. As a major sponsor, it will be able to use the marathon's name and logo for advertising prior to the race. The company is bringing out a special line of running shoes for the event.

BALTIMORE - A lawyer for a group of clients who received heart valves manufactured by Phase Pharmaceuticals has filed a lawsuit claiming the company knew that the valves were good for only 5 years and would have to be replaced, even though the literature describing the product claims that the valves will last 20 years.

PHOENIX - An increase in population in states in the Southwest has meant more profits for businesses that supply products and services in that area. Businesses that have profited the most by this migration to warmer states have been the building industry and utilities (particularly companies that use solar power to generate electricity). Other winners in the population explosion are companies that supply fuel for cars.

MALIBU - Best Beach Wear, the one-time star in the garment industry, has admitted that it cannot regain its old leading position without an infusion of capital and new management. Todd Landlover and Walt Waterman will resign their positions as CEO and chairman of the board when the company is bought out by Beach Designs.

Trading Record

Name _____

Date _____

Security	Purchase shares - price	Sell shares - price	Total Price	Commission

Date _____

Security	Purchase shares - price	Sell shares - price	Total Price	Commission

Transfer records of all sales and purchases to your portfolio and cash reserve records.

Stock Portfolio

Name_____

Record the current price and value of each stock and the total value of your portfolio.

Date _____

Security	Number of Shares	Price/Share	Total Value

Total Portfolio Value_____

Date _____

Security	Number of Shares	Price/Share	Total Value

Total Portfolio Value_____

At the end of the game, add the value of your total stock portfolio on the last trading day to the amount in your cash reserve account to get your total net worth.

Cash Reserve

Name _____

Day 1

beginning balance   *$ 50,000.00*

purchases (–)   _____

commission (–)   _____

balance   _____

Day 2

beginning balance   _____

sales (+)   _____

purchases (–)   _____

commission (–)   _____

balance   _____

Day 3

beginning balance   _____

sales (+)   _____

purchases (–)   _____

commission (–)   _____

balance   _____

Day 4

beginning balance   _____

sales (+)   _____

purchases (–)   _____

commission (–)   _____

balance   _____

Day 5

beginning balance   _____

sales (+)   _____

purchases (–)   _____

commission (–)   _____

balance   _____

At the end of the game add this amount to the value of your total stock portfolio to get your total net worth.

The Stock Market Game
Long Version

Overview

If you choose this longer version of the Stock Market Game you should be willing to follow the stock market over a period of two to three months. Once students have been introduced to the mechanics of the game and have chosen their initial stocks, you need not spend time every day to monitor and trade stocks. In fact, it is probably preferable to allow students to trade stocks only once or twice a week. Daily changes in stock prices are usually very small; therefore, students would see very little change in the prices of the stocks they own or the total value of their portfolios if they checked prices and traded on a daily basis. Over a period of time, you should see a movement in the prices as the market responds to economic and political events. By trading less frequently, students will better be able to see how events in the news affect stock prices.

In this version of the Stock Market Game, students will choose actual stocks that are listed on the New York Stock Exchange or the NASDAQ. To begin the game, you will give them a listing of stocks from which to choose. Brief descriptions of the stocks begins on page 54 and may be duplicated and distributed to students. An address is listed for each stock. Before you actually begin the simulation, you should have students write or e-mail and ask for the companies' annual reports. Information about each company can also be downloaded from the company's website on the Internet. If these stocks are not listed in your local newspaper, you may wish to purchase a *Wall Street Journal* or a newspaper from a larger city on the days you quote stock prices. Prices are also available on the Internet.

These companies were selected because they are solid companies, are companies that are likely to be listed in most newspapers, and are, for the large part, companies that young

people know something about. You may wish, however, to add or substitute other companies that reflect your specific objectives or a regional perspective. Just be sure that you have access to the stock prices for these companies. After the initial round of purchases, you may choose to let students select stocks of their own choosing. If students choose other stocks, they should know something about the company and should be encouraged to write for the company's annual report. Addresses for most businesses can be found in the reference section of the public library in books such as *Walker's Manual of Unlisted Stocks, Moody's Handbook of Common Stocks, Standard and Poor's Register of Corporations,* or *Hoover's Handbook of American Business,* or on the Internet.

Procedure

Day 1

1. Give students the company profiles and go through the listings as a class or in small groups. Ask students to think about which of these stocks would be good to own and why.

2. Review the rules for the game. The rules are:
- Students will start with $50,000. They can spend less than $50,000, but they cannot spend more that $50,000. Any money that they do not invest in stocks will remain in their cash reserve (which is like putting it in the bank until they need it).
- They have to own at least three different stocks.
- They have to buy and sell in multiples of 100.
- They cannot own more than 500 shares of any one stock.
- Each trading period they have to sell a minimum of 100 shares. They may sell more than

100 shares. These 100 shares may be only a portion of a stock they own. For example, if one of the students owns 500 shares of stock A, she may decide to sell only 100 shares of the 500 shares she owns. She could, however, decide to sell more than 100 shares.

- Each trading day they have to buy 100 shares of a stock other than the one they sold. They can, however, buy more shares of a stock they already own. For instance, they may own 200 shares of McDonald's and purchase 100 shares more.
- They will pay a 3% commission for all sales and purchases.
- Money that is not invested in stocks will be held in a cash reserve account. When stocks are sold, the money from the sales goes into the cash reserve account. They can never spend more money than they have in the cash account to buy new stocks. They cannot borrow money or spend more than they have.
- After the first trading day, they may choose one stock other than the ones that are suggested. They must know something about this company, and it must be listed in the newspaper that you will use to supply stock prices. Each person can own only one self-selected stock at a time. That one stock must be sold before buying another self-selected stock.
- All sales and purchases will be recorded on the Trading Record and then transferred to the Stock Portfolio and Cash Reserve sheets.
- The Trading Record, Stock Portfolio and Cash Reserve sheets will then be placed in the student's folder and handed in for you to keep until the next trading day.

3. Pass out folders and one copy each of the Trading Record, the Stock Portfolio, and the Cash Reserve sheets.

4. Review how to figure the total price for stocks (price x number of shares) and the commission (total price x .03).

5. If you did not do the short version of the Stock Market Game, review how to record sales and purchases and how to maintain up-to-date information on the Stock Portfolio

and Cash Reserve record sheets. Use pages 61 to 63 for examples.

6. Post stock prices. Using the form on page 60, provide a list of the most current prices for the stocks students will be using for their initial purchases.

7. Ask students to study the company profiles and the listed prices and then select stocks they would like to purchase. When they have selected their stocks, they should record their purchases on the Trading Record and then on the Stock Portfolio and Cash Reserve sheets.

Record Keeping

Pages 61 through 63 show how to use the record sheets to keep track of stock trading. When students buy or sell stocks, they will first record their transactions on the **Trading Record**. In the example, four stocks have been purchased on the first day, and the owner has recorded the number of shares that were purchased and the price per share. The number of shares was then multiplied by the price to obtain the total price (200 x $56.50 for Company ABC). Then the total price was multiplied by 3% to get the commission. The total commission for the four purchases was $1,243.88. On the second day, 200 shares of ABC were sold and 200 shares of GHI and 400 shares of MNO were purchased. The prices were recorded in the appropriate columns (either purchase or sell) and the commission was calculated as before. The total commission for these transactions was calculated. The total commission for the purchases and liquidations was $711.75

After students have decided on the stocks they want to buy and sell and recorded them on the Trading Records, they will use the **Stock Portfolio** to keep an up-to-date list of stocks that they own. In the example on page 62, the first day reflects the four stocks that were purchased, the number of shares of each stock, the price per share, and the total value. This information was basically copied from the Trading Record. The total value of the four stocks was added to get the total value of the portfolio, $41,462.50. On the second day of trading, the stock portfolio shows that all the shares of ABC have been sold, the price per share of DEF, GHI and JKL have been updated and the purchases of GHI and MNO have been recorded. The number of shares for each stock was multiplied by the number of shares owned to get the total value for each stock. The total values for the four stocks were then added to get a portfolio total of $43,650.00.

The **Cash Reserve** record sheet is where students keep track of money that they do not have invested in the stock market. On page 63 is an example of how to keep track of the cash reserves. This account shows a beginning balance of $50,000.00. The sum of the purchases for the first day ($41,462.50) and the commission ($1,243.88) were subtracted from the beginning balance to give a balance in the cash reserve of $7,293.62. This balance is brought down to become the beginning balance on day two. Since this trader sold 200 shares of ABC on the second day, the proceeds from this sale are added to the beginning balance. If a subtotal were done at this point, it would reflect a total in the cash reserves of $19,068.62. This is the amount that was available for the purchase of more stock. The trader bought 200 more shares of GHI and 400 shares of MNO. The total for these two purchases ($11,950.00) and the commission on the purchases and sales was subtracted from the balance to give a balance at the end of day two of $6,406.87. This amount became the beginning balance on day three.

Subsequent Trading Days

1. Post prices and the amount of change from the previous trading day's prices for the listed stocks. You can make a transparency of page 61 and show the prices on an overhead. Provide prices for students' self-selected stocks.

2. If any news events can be traced to rises or falls in stock prices, discuss these events and their effects.

3. Have students decide what stocks they will sell and what stocks they will add. They have to sell a minimum of 100 shares and buy a minimum of 100 shares. Remind them that they cannot spend more money than they have and they cannot own more than 500 shares of any one stock.

4. Have students record their purchases and sales on the Trading Record and make a new Stock Portfolio that reflects their current holdings. Have them record the money transactions on the Cash Reserve sheet.

5. Collect student folders containing all record sheets and hold them until the next trading day. During that time, check their transactions and calculations.

6. If you have access to the Internet, have students learn how to find stock prices and check company information on the Internet. Share any news releases that are posted on any of the companies' websites that might affect stock prices.

Last Day of the Simulation

1. Post prices for the twelve stocks. Provide prices from the newspaper or Internet for students' self-selected stocks.

2. There will be no trading this day.

3. Have students figure the value of their portfolios and record them on their Stock Portfolio sheets. Then have them add the amount of money in their cash reserve account to the value of their portfolios to get a total net worth.

4. Have each person figure out how much his or her portfolio has increased or decreased during the game. Discuss the strategies used by the people who made the greatest gains.

Rules

- You will start with $50,000. You can spend less than $50,000 but you cannot spend more than $50,000.

- You have to own at least three different stocks.

- You have to buy and sell in multiples of 100.

- You cannot own more than 500 shares of any one stock.

- Each trading period you have to sell a minimum of 100 shares.

- Each trading day you have to buy 100 shares of a stock other than the one you sold.

- You will pay a 3% commission for all sales and purchases.

- The money that you do not invest in stocks will be held in a cash reserve account (which is like putting it in the bank until you need it). When stocks are sold, the money from the sales goes into the cash reserve account. You can never spend more money than you have in the cash account to buy new stocks.

- After the first trading day, you may choose to own one stock other than the ones that are supplied by your teacher. You must know something about the company and the company must be listed in the newspaper that your teacher uses to supply stock prices. You can only own one self-selected stock at a time.

Company Profiles

American Greetings

1 American Road, Cleveland, OH 44144-2398
NYSE: AM; phone (216) 252-7300; website: http://www.amgreetings.com
Founded in 1906, American Greetings is an international manufacturer of greeting cards, gift wrap, party goods, stationery, gift items, picture frames, and other related items. The bulk of its sales is from greeting cards. It operates plants in the United States, Canada, United Kingdom, Mexico, and France. The company's products are distributed through a network of retail outlets, including drug stores and supermarkets. It licenses its greeting cards and artwork in 73 countries and in 23 languages.

Bristol-Meyers Squibb

345 Park Ave., New York, NY 10154
NYSE: BMY; phone (212) 546-4000; website: http://www.bms.com
Bristol-Meyers Squibb is a leading supplier of health and personal care products that include prescription drugs, over-the-counter preparations, infant formulas, orthopedic implants, and health and beauty aids. Some of its brands include Ban, Bufferin, Comtrex, Clairol, Enfamil, Excedrin, and Nuprin. All four of the company's divisions (pharmaceuticals, medical devices, consumer products, and nutrition) have shown strong sales, and each division has a large line of high-quality products.

Campbell Soup

Campbell Place, Camden, NJ 08103-1799
NYSE: CPB; phone (856) 342-4800; website: http://www.campbellsoup.com
Campbell Soup started in 1869 as a canned food processor. In 1897 the company made its first condensed soup and it has been successfully marketing its soups ever since. The company also manufactures Swanson frozen dinners, Mrs. Paul's frozen fish, Open Pit barbecue sauce, Franco-American, Prego, V8 vegetable juice, Pepperidge Farm baked goods, Godiva chocolates, and Campbell's Pork and Beans. One division of the company provides food services to restaurants, hospitals, and schools. The company markets its products around the globe.

Chevron Texaco

575 Market St., San Francisco, CA 94105
NYSE: CVX; phone (415) 894-7700; website: http://www.chevrontexaco.com
Chevron Texaco is a worldwide petroleum company with interests in chemicals and minerals. It is a leading domestic producer of crude oil and natural gas and refines and markets refined oil products like gasoline, lubricants, asphalt, and chemicals. It is the largest refiner in the United States, but it is also active in overseas exploration, production, refining, and marketing. Chevron Texaco also mines and markets coal.

Eli Lilly

Eli Lily Corporation Center, Indianapolis, IN 46285
NYSE: LLY; phone (317) 276-2000; website: http://www.lilly.com
Eli Lilly is one of the worlds foremost health care companies. It is a leader in development of prescription drugs. It also produces products for animal health and agricultural use. Its biggest selling drug is Prozac, a drug used for treating depression. The company does business in 120 countries. The company's focus is on discovering, developing, manufacturing, and marketing innovative medicines.

General Electric

3135 Easton Turnpike, Fairfield, CT 06828-0001
NYSE: GE; phone (203) 373-2211; website: http://www.ge.com
Though this company can trace its origins back to Thomas Edison, who invented the light bulb in 1879, it was actually founded in 1892. Since that time, it has enlarged the scope of its business dealings. General Electric is the largest electrical equipment manufacturer. Its business includes making jet engines, industrial products, appliances, power systems and technical products. It also owns NBC Broadcasting and has a branch that provides financial services. Its overseas sales account for over one-third of its business.

Hewlett-Packard

3000 Hanover Street, Palo Alto, CA 94304
NYSE: HWP; phone (650) 857-1501; website: http://www.hp.com
Hewlett-Packard designs, manufactures, and services electronic products and systems for computing and communications. Its products are used in industry, business, engineering, science, medicine, and education. It has over 23,000 products that include computers and peripherals, electronic test and measurement instruments and systems, networking products, medical equipment, instruments for chemical analysis, calculators, and electronic components. While it is a large American corporation, 60% of its business is done outside of the United States. Most of its revenues come from sales of computer products and services.

Intel

2200 Mission College Blvd., Santa Clara, CA 95052
NASDAQ: INTC; phone (408) 765-8080; website: http://www.intel.com
Intel designs, develops, manufacturers, and markets advanced microcomputer components and related products. The company made its first microprocessor in 1971 and remains a world leader in making microprocessors (the part of a computer that processes data and controls other devices). It sells computer components and chips to computer manufacturers and offers PC users products that expand their computers' capabilities (such as networking devices). Over half of its sales are overseas.

McDonald's

One McDonald's Plaza, Oak Brook, IL 60521
NYSE: MCD; phone (630) 623-3000; website: http://www.mcdonalds.com
McDonald's is the largest and best-known food service company in the world. It has over 21,000 locations in over 80 countries. McDonald's restaurants serve a menu of moderately priced foods. Despite its huge size, on any given day the company serves only a very small percentage of the world's population, thus the company feels there is plenty of room for growth. The company has been steadily opening operations in other countries and continues to open new locations in the United States. It is also opening restaurants in unusual spots such as high school cafeterias, hospitals, gas stations, and inside large discount stores.

PepsiCo

700 Anderson Hill Rd., Purchase, NY 10577
NYSE: PEP; phone (914) 253-2000; website: http://www.pepsico.com
PepsiCo is a leading producer of products in the snack food, soft drink, and restaurant food industries. It is the world's second largest soft drink company (including Pepsi Cola, Diet Pepsi, and Mountain Dew), but also operates restaurants (Pizza Hut, KFC, and Taco Bell), and markets snack foods (Frito-Lay). The restaurants and snack food divisions have produced impressive sales and growth for the company. The company distributes snack foods in 40 countries.

Sara Lee

3 First National Plaza, Chicago IL 60602
NYSE: SLE; phone (312) 726-2600; website: http://www.saralee.com
Sara Lee is a manufacturer and marketer of a wide variety of products worldwide. Its products are sold in 140 countries, with sales in those countries accounting for 40% of its revenues. Its products include hosiery, packaged meats, coffee, underwear and active wear, shoe care products, and bakery items. The company's largest brands include Hanes, Sara Lee, Hillshire Farms, Jimmy Dean, L'Eggs, and Playtex, plus a number of brand name products in other countries. It is a major food company in Europe and Japan.

Wal-Mart Stores

702 SW 8th St., Bentonville, AR 72716
NYSE: WMT; phone (501) 273-4000; website: http://www.wal-mart.com
Wal-Mart is the largest retailer in the world, operating some 2,000 discount stores, close to 500 Sam's Wholesale Clubs, and over 200 Supercenters. It also has stores in Canada, Asia and Mexico. Wal-Mart stores offer low prices, high value, and customer service. It has an efficient distribution system and has consistently maintained low prices for its customers. The company is continually looking for ways to expand and open new stores. In the past, the stores have reported solid financial growth. Wal-Mart discount stores have consistently outpaced other discount chains.

Trading Record

Name _____

Date _____

Security	Purchase shares - price	Sell shares - price	Total Price	Commission

Date _____

Security	Purchase shares - price	Sell shares - price	Total Price	Commission

Transfer records of all sales and purchases to your portfolio and cash reserve records.

Stock Portfolio

Name_____

Record the current price and value of each stock and the total value of your portfolio.

Date _____

Security	Number of Shares	Price/Share	Total Value

Total Portfolio Value_____

Date _____

Security	Number of Shares	Price/Share	Total Value

Total Portfolio Value_____

At the end of the game, add the value of your total stock portfolio on the last trading day to the amount in your cash reserve account to get your total net worth.

Cash Reserve

Name _____

Date _____

      beginning balance   *$50,000.00*

      purchases (–)   _____

      commission (–)   _____

      balance   _____

Date _____

      beginning balance   _____

      sales (+)   _____

      purchases (–)   _____

      commission (–)   _____

      balance   _____

Date _____

      beginning balance   _____

      sales (+)   _____

      purchases (–)   _____

      commission (–)   _____

      balance   _____

Date _____

      beginning balance   _____

      sales (+)   _____

      purchases (–)   _____

      commission (–)   _____

      balance   _____

Date _____

      beginning balance   _____

      sales (+)   _____

      purchases (–)   _____

      commission (–)   _____

      balance   _____

Date _____

      beginning balance   _____

      sales (+)   _____

      purchases (–)   _____

      commission (–)   _____

      balance   _____

Date _____

      beginning balance   _____

      sales (+)   _____

      purchases (–)   _____

      commission (–)   _____

      balance   _____

Daily Stock Prices

Date_____

Company	Symbol	price/share	change
American Greetings	AM		
Bristol-Meyers Squibb	BMY		
Campbell Soup	CPB		
Chevron	CVX		
Eli Lilly	LLY		
General Electric	GE		
Hewlett-Packard	HWP		
Intel	INTC		
McDonald's	MCD		
PepsiCo	PEP		
Sara Lee	SLE		
Wal-Mart	WMT		

Trading Record

Name _Example_

Date _Day 1_

Security	Purchase shares - price	Sell shares - price	Total Price	Commission 3%
ABC	200 / 56.50		$11,300.00	$339.00
DEF	400 / 14.125		$5,650.00	$169.50
GHI	300 / 27.375		$8,212.50	$246.38
JKL	400 / 40.75		$16,300.00	$489.00

$1,243.88

Date _Day 2_

Security	Purchase shares - price	Sell shares - price	Total Price	Commission 3%
ABC		200 / 58.875	$11,775.00	$353.25
GHI	400 / 29.50		$5,900.00	$177.00
MNO	400 / 15.125		$6,050.00	$181.50

$711.75

Transfer records of all sales and purchases to your portfolio and cash reserve records.

Stock Portfolio

Name __Example__

Record the current price and value of each stock and the total value of your portfolio.

Date __Day 1__

Security	Number of Shares	Price/Share	Total Value
ABC	200	56.50	$11,300.00
DEF	400	14.125	$5,650.00
GHI	300	27.375	$8,212.50
JKL	400	40.75	$16,300.00

Total Portfolio Value __$41,462.50__

Date __Day 2__

Security	Number of Shares	Price/Share	Total Value
ABC	0		
DEF	400	14.75	$5,900.00
GHI	500	29.50	$14,750.00
JKL	400	42.375	$16,950.00
MNO	400	15.125	$6,050.00

Total Portfolio Value __$43,650.00__

At the end of the game, add the value of your total stock portfolio on the last trading day to the amount in your cash reserve account to get your total net worth.

Cash Reserve

Name *Example*

Day 1

beginning balance	$ 50,000.00
purchases (–)	– 41,462.50
commission (–)	– 1,243.88
balance	$7,293.62

Day 2

beginning balance	$7,293.62
sales (+)	+11,775.00
purchases (–)	–11,950.00
commission (–)	–711.75
balance	$6,406.87

Day 3

beginning balance	$6,406.87
sales (+)	
purchases (–)	
commission (–)	
balance	

Day 4

beginning balance	
sales (+)	
purchases (–)	
commission (–)	
balance	

Day 5

beginning balance	
sales (+)	
purchases (–)	
commission (–)	
balance	

At the end of the game add this amount to the value of your total stock portfolio to get your total net worth.

Answers

Stock Phrases, page 8

investor	NASDAQ
stocks	Stock Exchanges
dividends	price
stockbroker	shares
diversify	commission
portfolio	portfolio
bear	split
blue chip	investor

Figuring Prices, page 13

1. 11,350
2. 4,750
3. 16,125
4. 27,825
5. 7,512.50
6. 8,062.50
7. 24,950
8. 16,750
9. 21,300
10. 9,550
11. 2,562.50
12. 2,175
13. 9,100
14. 53,656.25
15. Answers will vary.

Prices and Events, page 14

1. SunCitrus (+)
2. Hip Hop (+)
3. Biotec (−)
4. ChocoBear (+)
5. Banana Computers (−)
6. Global Communications (+)
7. Hip Hop (+), ChocoBear (+) SunCitrus (+)
   Banana Computers (−),
   maybe Global Communication (−)

Reading Stock Prices, page 16

1. 19.75
2. KLM
3. ABC, PQR, KLM
4. XYZ
5. 58.5
6. 105.375

   @ANSWERS = 7. 16.75

8. 45
9. 104.5
10. KLM
11. STU

Making Money with Stocks, page 19

1. initial investment - $4650.00
   sale - $4025.00
   loss - $625.00
2. initial investment - $10,850.00
   dividends - $800.00
   sale price -$13,300.00
   profit - $3.250.00
3. initial investment - $675.00
   dividends - $600.00
   sale price -$1,262.50
   profit - $1,187.50

Buy or Sell?, page 20

A . 7/20/96,   10/3/97, $9.50, $950.00
B. 1/31/97,   6/4/97, $2.125, $212.50
C . 9/3/96,   3/17/97, $7.50, $750.00
D . 6/15/95,   11/12/96, $5.75, $575.00
E . 11/12/96, 6/4/97, $5.50, $550.00
F . 6/15/95,   10/3/97, $5.125, $512.50

Charting Prices, page 21

Answers will vary

Which Exchange?, page 23

Closing prices will vary depending on the date when the
   prices are read.

Costco - NASDAQ	Macromedia - NASDAQ
Xerox - NYSE	Wendys - NYSE
Lincare - NASDAQ	Applebee's - NASDAQ
American Airlines - NYSE	Intel - NASDAQ
Nike - NYSE	

Figuring Commission, page 28

1. 400 x 59.25 x .03 = $711.00
2. 500 x 48 x .04 = $960.00
3. [9100 x 39.625) + (100 x 26.375)] x .05
   (3962.50 + 2637.50)x .05 = $330.00
4. [(200 x 46.50) + (100 x 26.375)] x .05
   (9300.00 + 4150.00) x .04 = $538.00
5. 500 x 37.75 x .03 = $566.25
6. [(500 x 109.125) + (300 x 112.25) + (100 x 33.375)]
   91575.00 x .05 = $4578.75

Buying Stock, page 29

Answers will vary.

The Right Choice, page 31

Answers will vary.

Common Core State Standards Alignment

Grade	Common Core State Standards in Math
Grade 4	4.OA.A Use the four operations with whole numbers to solve problems.
	4.NBT.A Generalize place value understanding for multi-digit whole numbers.
	4.NBT.B Use place value understanding and properties of operations to perform multi-digit arithmetic.
	4.NF.C Understand decimal notation for fractions, and compare decimal fractions.
	4.MD.B Represent and interpret data.
Grade 5	5.NBT.A Understand the place value system.
	5.NBT.B Perform operations with multi-digit whole numbers and with decimals to hundredths.
Grade 6	6.NS.B Compute fluently with multi-digit numbers and find common factors and multiples.
	6.NS.C Apply and extend previous understandings of numbers to the system of rational numbers.
Grade 7	7.RP.A Analyze proportional relationships and use them to solve real-world and mathematical problems.
	7.NS.A Apply and extend previous understandings of operations with fractions.
	7.EE.B Solve real-life and mathematical problems using numerical and algebraic expressions and equations.
Key: OA=Operations & Algebraic Thinking; NBT=Number & Operations in Base Ten; NF=Number & Operations—Fractions; MD=Measurement & Data; RP=Ratios & Proportional Relationships; NS=The Number System; EE=Expressions & Equations	

Printed in the United States
by Baker & Taylor Publisher Services